# How to keep my healthy and safe

Author:
**Kyra Lüthi**

Co-author and Illustrator:
**Ysabel Lindo**

ISBN 9798513407447

This book is currently available in several languages. If you wish to connect with us, please visit our website at www.breakingsilencemvmt.org.

# Author's Note

Dear parents & teachers,

I am writing to you as a gender-based violence (GBV) survivor, a parent and an educator. It is important for our kids to learn about their physical well-being which means keeping their body healthy and safe. At the early age of childhood, we teach them how to do potty, wash their hands, eat fruits and vegetables, and exercise daily. But more often than not, we tend to forget to teach them how to keep their body safe.

As a GBV survivor at the age of nine, I would not want any of our children to go through what I experienced. I was unaware of body safety; so if only I knew then that what happened to me was wrong, a lot of things could have been stopped.

As an educator, I strongly believe that there is no better solution than education. When we inform our students about the basic rights of their body, respect and empowerment towards themselves and others will instinctively be produced.

As a parent, we are responsible for letting our children know about their bodies before it's too late. We are our children's main source of trust and knowledge about everything. Therefore, making "body safety" a normal thing to talk about in the house just like taking a bath, doing homework and sleeping on time, will have a stronger impact and influence on them.

As I understand that these things may sometimes be difficult to impose in a classroom or a household, this book is created to serve as a must-have guideline for every parent and teacher. Its simple yet vibrant illustrations, and personalized journal would be an entertaining way for you and your children or students to read and do together.

Prevention is our goal and we thank you for taking part in it.

Sincerely,
Kyra Lüthi
Author & Founder
Breaking Silence Movement

Hello! My name is
_____!
And this is how
I keep my body
healthy.

# Every day,
# I take a shower,

I change clothes,

# I eat healthy food,

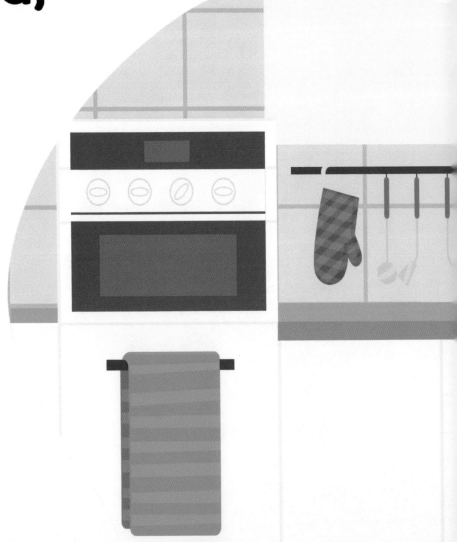

# and I exercise.

# But how do I keep my body safe?

# My body has
# red zones.

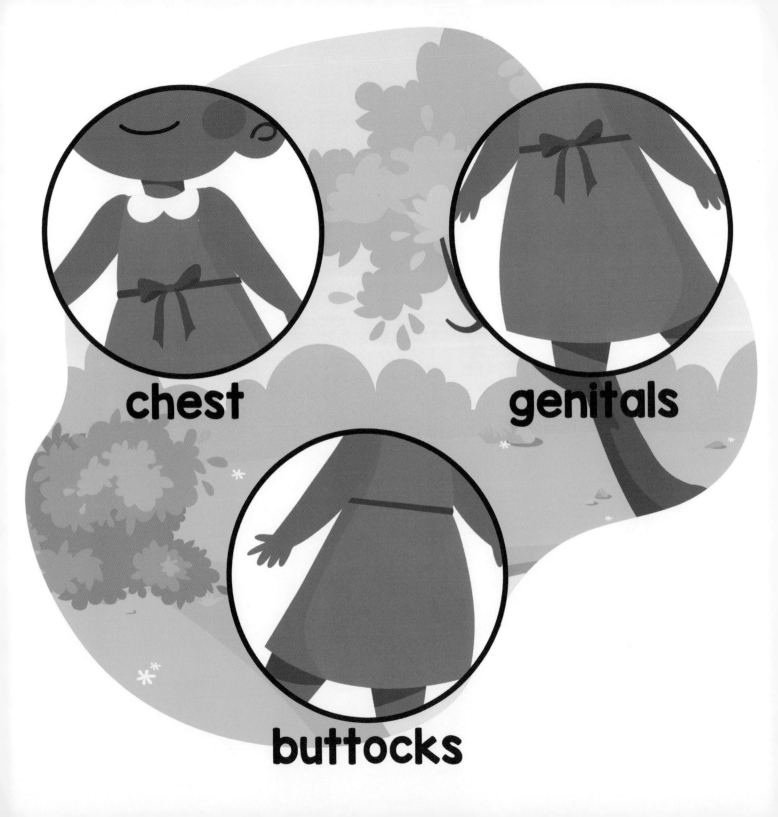

chest

genitals

buttocks

Red zones
are the
private parts
of my body.

# My red zones should not be touched by other people.

My red zones should also not be seen by other people.

If someone wants
to see or touch
my red zones,
I need to say:

If someone wants me to see or touch their red zones, I need to say:

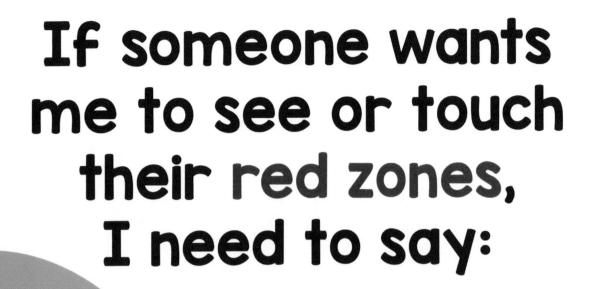

NO!

I should also tell my parents and teachers about it so they can protect me.

And that's how
I keep my
body healthy
and safe!

# My Body Safety Journal

paste your
photo here

Hello! My name is

_____!

I am

____ years old.

# Do I keep my body healthy?

(Draw a check mark inside the box of the things you do to keep your body healthy)

☐ take a shower

☐ change clothes

☐ eat healthy food

☐ exercise

# Do I keep my body safe?

# Where are my red zones?

(Draw red circles on the red zones)

Should other people see and touch my red zones?

_____

Should I see or touch other people's red zones?

_____

Who should I talk to if someone wants to see and touch my red zones?

_____

_____

**What should I say if someone wants to see or touch my red zones?**
(Write your answer inside the speech bubble)

# What should I say if someone wants to show me or asks me to touch their red zones?
(Write your answer inside the speech bubble)

# My Body Safety Mantra

I love my body,
And my body loves me.
My body belongs to me,
and nobody can see or touch it but me.
I have to be brave to say NO,
when someone wants to see or touch
my private zones.

# Guidelines for adults when kids start to talk:

The adult's response to the trauma experienced by a child plays a vital role. It can have as much more impact on the child as the incident itself. It is the adult's responsibility to know how to process the incident when a child reports it.

Here are some guidelines on what to do and ask:

1. Reassure the child that what happened is not their fault and that you believe everything they reported to you.

2. If they are ready to explain more of the details, you may start by asking these questions:
   • What happened?
   • When did it happen?
   • How many times did it happen?
   • Where did it happen?
   • With who?

3. Applaud the child for being brave and courageous for telling you what happened.

4. Even if there is no physical injury, it is important that they get medical attention right away. To have an official medical record, consider reporting to the authorities immediately.

5. Ensure the child that they are safe and that you will protect them.

6. Get in touch with local resources who can provide counseling and therapy.

7. It is important to take note that it will not be possible for your child to return to the way they were before the assault. The best thing you can do is to constantly express to your child your support and belief in them so they can heal as soon as possible. In case it is too difficult for you as a parent to handle it, you must also consider taking therapy to cope with the trauma and normalize the healing process.


*If you are a teacher, you must inform the parents of the child right away and encourage them to report the incident to the authorities immediately. In most countries, teachers, or other people regarded as witnesses are allowed to call on the police to report an incident even if they are indirectly involved, especially if they believe that the child's safety is at risk.

**Breaking Silence Movement** fights the issue of *domestic and sexual assault* through creating awareness, empowerment, preventive and educational strategies. It also aims to empower survivors and victims by providing support needed upon their different cases and situations such as psychological, legal, financial and most importantly, educational and professional opportunities.

It is a private, non-profit organization based in Manila, Philippines, and with project operations in France, Switzerland and United States of America. It started out as an independent volunteer group in 2010 headed by *Ms. Kyra Lüthi*. The group held numerous outreach projects in the Philippines initially for the benefit of the underprivileged children, and overseas as the Philippine representative in a number of charity events. As the founder's vision continues to expand, she is drawn to a cause that is very close to her own personal story. Being a survivor, she has decided to make it her life commitment to exert her efforts into putting an end to domestic and sexual assault.

# About the Authors

## Kyra Luthi
### Author

Kyra is an entrepreneur, author and humanitarian. She has a business background in life, wealth and asset management with operations mainly in Europe, Asia and the USA. She is currently writing about wealth, business and psychosociology in the form of theoretical articles.

In the beginning of her career, she founded a creative and events company and a Personality Development Workshop Program that incorporates positive psychology in its modules; both start-ups were operated in the Philippines. The educational program has sparked her interest into amplifying the awareness and preventive information needed for her advocacy against domestic and sexual violence.

She has been a humanitarian at an early age, representing street children from the Philippines and voluntarily raising funds for their financial and educational needs. As a survivor, it has became her life commitment to exert her skills to fulfilling a world free of domestic and sexual violence through prevention - leading her to founding Breaking Silence Movement.

## Ysabel Lindo
### Co-author and Illustrator

Ysabel is an educator, author, and artist based in Manila, Philippines. She graduated with a Bachelor's Degree in Elementary Childhood Education from De La Salle University - Manila, and has completed Introduction to Psychology course from Yale University. She has been an educator for nine years, and has written five books for a leveled preschool reading program. She started as a teacher for preschool students and kids with special needs, and later on became a Trainer for preschool teachers from a reputable international school in the Asia Pacific. Currently, she works as a Curriculum Consultant.

She believes that through teaching, she found her *"Ikigai"* - a Japanese concept meaning "a reason for being" or "doing what you're good at, doing what the world needs, doing what you love, and doing what you can be paid for".

In her spare time, she likes to tap into her creativity through graphic designing, sketching and painting murals; and seek fulfilling work such as volunteering for charity.

Printed in Great Britain
by Amazon